CW01429841

# Earthing Explained: A Beginner's Guide to Grounding and Its Benefits

Stephen W. Bradeley BSc. (Hons)

# Table of Contents

# About myself

My name is Stephen Bradeley, and I am based in the United Kingdom. I hold a Bachelor of Science (Honours) degree in Sports Science from Staffordshire University, where I studied during the 1990s. My academic focus was on exercise for health, with a particular emphasis on hypokinetic diseases. For my dissertation, I explored aspects of breast cancer, a subject that has personal significance for me.

During my time at university, I developed a keen interest in breast cancer research due to my family's diagnosis as carriers of the BRCA2 gene. The BRCA2 gene is a tumour suppressor, and mutations within this gene can markedly increase the risk of developing certain cancers, especially breast and ovarian cancer. Mutations in BRCA2, as well as BRCA1, are key contributors to hereditary breast and ovarian cancer syndrome (HBOC).

Unfortunately, two of my sisters were diagnosed with breast cancer at a young age, which further deepened my commitment to this field.

More recently, my interest has expanded to include grounding—or earthing—as a potential intervention for inflammatory diseases. This book aims to provide readers with a foundational understanding of grounding, its principles, and its possible benefits, particularly in relation to inflammation and overall health.

# INTRODUCTION TO EARTHING

**Earthing Explained: A Beginner's Guide to Grounding and Its Benefits**

# Introduction:  What is Grounding / Earthing

Earthing, also known as grounding, is the practice of connecting oneself to the Earth's surface electrons by direct contact with the ground or through conductive systems such as mats, sheets, bracelets and earthing rods. This concept is rooted in the idea that the Earth's surface has a vast reservoir of free electrons that can neutralize free radicals and reduce electrical imbalances within the body, potentially leading to health benefits. Advocates believe that modern lifestyles—characterized by frequent use of insulated shoes, synthetic clothing, and indoor environments—create a disconnect from the Earth's natural energy, which may contribute to inflammation, stress, fatigue, and various chronic health issues. Earthing is thought to promote better sleep, reduce pain, improve blood flow, and enhance overall well-being by restoring the body's electrical balance. Scientifically, grounding works by allowing the transfer of electrons from the Earth into the body, which can neutralize reactive oxygen species and decrease inflammation.

Techniques for grounding include walking barefoot on natural surfaces like grass, sand, or soil, or using grounding devices such as mats and sheets connected to the Earth's ground. While some scientific studies support claims of improved sleep and reduced inflammation, the field remains somewhat controversial, with ongoing research required to substantiate many of the health benefits claimed by proponents. Nonetheless, grounding is generally considered a safe and simple practice that encourages physical contact with the natural environment, fostering a sense of connection and well-being. It emphasizes the importance of reconnecting with nature in a modern world increasingly dominated by electronic devices and artificial surfaces, offering a potentially easy and cost-effective way to enhance health and vitality.

# Brief history and origins

The history and origins of Earthing, also known as grounding, trace back to ancient civilizations that recognized the healing and restorative properties of direct contact with the Earth. Throughout history, various cultures have incorporated practices that involved walking barefoot, sitting directly on the ground, or using natural materials in rituals and daily life to promote health and spiritual well-being. For example, indigenous tribes across Africa, Asia, and the Americas have long valued the grounding experience, believing that connecting with the Earth restores balance and harmony within the body and mind. In ancient Greece, the concept of "harmony with nature" was central to philosophies of well-being, and practitioners often sought direct contact with natural surfaces to attain health benefits. Similarly, in traditional Chinese medicine, the Earth element and its energetic influence are fundamental principles, emphasizing the importance of grounding for vitality and balance.

The formal scientific exploration of grounding as a health practice, however, emerged more recently in the 20th century, amid a growing awareness of the impact of modern lifestyle and technology on human health. During the 1960s and 1970s, researchers and health enthusiasts began to investigate the potential benefits of electrical grounding, especially as the proliferation of insulated footwear, synthetic clothing, and indoor living created a disconnect from the Earth's natural energy. Pioneering work by scientists such as Dr. Gaétan Chevalier and Clint Ober in the late 20th and early 21st centuries helped to propel grounding into mainstream consciousness. Ober, a former cable television executive, became particularly influential after experiencing health improvements through barefoot walking and grounding devices, leading him to investigate the scientific basis of these effects. He and other researchers conducted studies to understand how direct contact with the

Earth's surface could influence electrical and biological processes within the body.

The modern understanding of grounding also gained momentum through the development of specialized products, such as grounding mats, sheets, and conductive footwear, designed to facilitate safe and consistent contact with the Earth's energy indoors or when outdoor access is limited. These innovations were coupled with growing scientific interest in bioelectrical physiology, inflammation, and oxidative stress, providing a framework for understanding how grounding might influence health. Over the past two decades, grounding has transitioned from a fringe theory to a recognized area of alternative health practices, supported by scientific studies, anecdotal reports, and a burgeoning community of practitioners. Despite ongoing debates and the need for further research, the core idea—that reconnecting with the Earth's natural electrical energy can promote healing—remains central to the practice's origin story. Today, grounding continues to be embraced by those seeking natural, holistic approaches to health, echoing its ancient roots while grounded in modern scientific inquiry.

# Why is this book for you why should I begin Earthing?

From this point on in the book we will refer to it as simply Earthing. Earthing and Grounding are one and the same thing. Reading a book about Earthing or grounding offers a compelling opportunity to explore a simple yet potentially transformative approach to enhancing your overall well-being. In an age where modern life often disconnects us from nature—dominated by concrete jungles, synthetic materials, and a relentless digital environment—learning about Earthing can inspire you to reconnect with the natural world in a meaningful way.

The practice is easy to incorporate into daily life; it requires no expensive equipment or complex routines, just a willingness to walk barefoot on natural surfaces or use grounding devices. A well-informed book can provide you with the scientific background, historical context, and practical tips needed to understand how grounding influences your body's electrical system, reduces inflammation, improves sleep, and boosts your energy levels. It can demystify the science behind the practice, showing how the Earth's electrons may neutralize free radicals and help your body restore its natural balance.

Moreover, reading about Earthing can broaden your perspective on health, emphasizing the importance of natural, holistic approaches that complement conventional medicine. It can motivate you to adopt healthier habits—like spending more time outdoors, walking barefoot, or creating a grounding routine—leading to tangible benefits such as decreased stress, reduced pain, and better mental clarity. The knowledge gained from such a book can empower you to take control of your health in a simple, accessible way, fostering a greater sense of connection to nature and yourself. Additionally, understanding the science and stories behind Earthing can inspire you to share this practice with loved ones, creating a ripple effect of health and vitality in your community. Ultimately, reading a book about Earthing is not just about learning a new technique; it's about opening yourself to a holistic lifestyle that nurtures your physical, emotional, and spiritual health, helping you feel more grounded, balanced, and alive in today's fast-paced world.

# Understanding the Basics of Electricity and the Human Body

# Chapter 1: Understanding the Basics of Electricity and the Human Body

## Basic concepts of electrical charge

Electrical charge is a fundamental property of matter that causes particles to exert forces on each other, either attracting or repelling, depending on whether they have opposite or like charges. In the context of Earth and its atmosphere, electrical charges play a crucial role in phenomena such as lightning and atmospheric electricity. The Earth itself acts as a giant electrical conductor, typically maintaining a negative charge relative to the ionosphere, which is positively charged. This charge imbalance creates an electric field that extends through the atmosphere. During thunderstorms, the movement of water droplets and ice particles within clouds causes separation of charges, leading to a build-up of electrical potential.

When this potential difference becomes large enough, it results in a sudden discharge of electricity—lightning—that equalizes the charge imbalance and releases the stored electrical energy as a bright flash and thunder. Understanding electrical charges in Earth's atmosphere is essential for comprehending weather phenomena, safety measures during storms, and the broader dynamics of atmospheric electricity.

Electrical charge is a fundamental property of matter that involves the presence and interaction of positive and negative electric charges. In the Earth's atmosphere, electrical charges play a vital role in phenomena such as lightning, which occurs when there is a significant imbalance of charge within clouds or between clouds and the ground. The Earth itself acts as a vast electrical conductor, generally maintaining a negative charge relative to the positively charged ionosphere. This creates an electric field that extends through the atmosphere, influencing weather patterns and electrical phenomena. During thunderstorms, the movement of water droplets, ice crystals, and other particles within clouds causes charge separation, with lighter, positively charged particles accumulating at the top of clouds and negatively charged particles gathering at the bottom. When the electric potential difference becomes large enough, it results in a discharge—lightning—that neutralizes the charge imbalance and releases vast amounts of electrical energy into the environment.

# Earthing Explained: A Beginner's Guide to Grounding and Its Benefits

This natural electrical activity is not just a spectacular display; it also has implications for human health and well-being. The concept of grounding, or earthing, involves direct contact with the Earth's surface—such as walking barefoot or using conductive systems connected to the ground—to facilitate the transfer of electrons between the Earth and the body. Proponents of grounding suggest that this practice helps neutralize excess free radicals in the body, which are associated with inflammation, oxidative stress, and various chronic diseases. When the body is grounded, it is believed that electrons from the Earth can enter the body, helping to stabilize electrical imbalances at a cellular level, reduce inflammation, and promote overall health.

Scientific studies on grounding have shown promising results, including reductions in pain, improved sleep, decreased stress, and enhanced immune function. The theory is that by reconnecting with the Earth's natural electrical charge, individuals can restore their body's natural electrical balance, counteracting the negative effects of electromagnetic pollution from modern technology.

In essence, grounding taps into the Earth's inherent electrical properties—its negative charge and the flow of electrons—to promote health and well-being. While more research is needed to fully understand and validate these claims, the connection between Earth's electrical charge, atmospheric phenomena, and human health highlights the profound influence of nature.

## How the human body conducts electricity

The human body is an intricate and highly organized system capable of conducting electricity, a fundamental process essential for various physiological functions. This electrical conduction is primarily due to the presence of ions, which are electrically charged particles, within body fluids such as blood, intracellular fluid, and extracellular fluid. These ions, including sodium ($Na+$), potassium ($K+$), calcium ($Ca2+$), magnesium ($Mg2+$), chloride ($Cl-$), and bicarbonate ($HCO3-$), create an environment that facilitates electrical conductivity. The human body's tissues and fluids act as an excellent medium for the movement of these ions, allowing electrical signals to be transmitted seamlessly across different systems.

One of the most critical aspects of electrical conduction in the human body is the nervous system. Neurons, or nerve cells, communicate through electrical impulses known as action potentials. These impulses are generated when specific ions move across the cell membranes of neurons through specialized protein channels. For example, when a neuron is stimulated, sodium channels open, allowing Na+ ions to rush into the cell, depolarizing the membrane and generating an electrical signal. Subsequently, potassium channels open to allow K+ ions to exit, restoring the resting state. This rapid exchange of ions propagates the electrical signal along the nerve fibre, enabling the transmission of sensory information, motor commands, and complex neural processes. This electrochemical signalling is fundamental to functions such as muscle contraction, reflexes, and brain activity.

Similarly, the heart's rhythmic contractions are driven by electrical signals generated within cardiac cells. Specialized pacemaker cells in the sinoatrial node produce rhythmic electrical impulses that spread through the heart muscle, causing coordinated contractions essential for pumping blood effectively. This electrical activity can be measured non-invasively through electrocardiograms (ECGs), which record the heart's electrical signals and are vital tools in diagnosing cardiac conditions.

Beyond the nervous and cardiovascular systems, the human body also conducts electricity through muscle tissues and other organs. Muscles respond to electrical stimuli by contracting, a process controlled by the nervous system. This electrical responsiveness is why electrical stimulation is used therapeutically for pain relief, muscle rehabilitation, and physical therapy.

The body's ability to conduct electricity depends heavily on the composition of bodily fluids and tissues, which act as conductive mediums. The presence of ions in body fluids ensures that electrical currents can flow efficiently. The skin, though a good insulator, can conduct electricity when moist or when electrical devices are applied directly to it, which forms the basis for techniques like electrotherapy.

In summary, the human body conducts electricity primarily through the movement of ions within its fluids and tissues. This conduction underpins vital physiological processes such as nerve signalling, muscle contraction, and heart rhythm regulation. Understanding how the body conducts electricity not only provides insights into normal bodily functions but also aids in diagnosing diseases, developing medical treatments, and exploring new therapeutic technologies that harness the body's electrical properties.

In Summary: At the core of the body's natural electrical balance lies the distribution and movement of charged particles—ions—across cell membranes and throughout bodily fluids, a finely tuned system that underpins nerve signalling, muscle contraction, cardiac rhythm, and metabolic regulation. In every cell, proteins embedded in the lipid bilayer act as ion channels and pumps—most notably the sodium-potassium ATPase —that establish and maintain an electrochemical gradient by actively transporting three sodium ions out and two potassium ions in, creating a resting membrane potential typically around −70 millivolts.

This voltage difference is essential for the generation of action potentials: when a stimulus triggers the opening of voltage-gated sodium channels, $Na^+$ rushes into the cell, depolarizing the membrane and propagating an electrical impulse along neurons; subsequent opening of potassium channels and $Na^+/K^+$ pump activity repolarize the cell, restoring the baseline potential and preparing it for the next signal. In the heart, specialized pacemaker cells in the sinoatrial node leverage similar ionic exchanges— through $Ca^{2+}$, $Na^+$, and $K^+$ channels—to generate rhythmic electrical impulses that coordinate atrial and ventricular contractions, a process continuously monitored and modulated by autonomic inputs to match the body's demands.

Muscle fibres themselves respond to motor neuron signals via acetylcholine-mediated depolarization, allowing $Ca^{2+}$ release from the sarcoplasmic reticulum and triggering actin-myosin cross-bridge cycling for contraction. Beyond rapid signalling, the body's overall electrical integrity depends on the balanced distribution of electrolytes in blood plasma, interstitial fluid, and intracellular fluid—fluids whose conductivity permits uniform electrical fields and efficient ion exchange—while insulating structures such as myelin sheaths and skin help direct current flow and protect delicate tissues. At the molecular level, redox reactions in mitochondria and throughout metabolic pathways involve the controlled transfer of electrons, another facet of electrical balance critical for ATP production and cellular homeostasis. Slight imbalances in ion concentrations or membrane potentials can manifest as symptoms—tingling, muscle weakness, arrhythmias, or neurological disturbances—thereby highlighting the importance of

16

electrolyte homeostasis, pH regulation, and adequate hydration. Emerging research also explores how external electromagnetic fields and practices like grounding may influence the body's electron equilibrium by allowing terrestrial electrons to neutralize free radicals, potentially reducing oxidative stress and inflammation. In sum, the human body conducts and regulates electricity through orchestrated ion movements, membrane potentials, and redox chemistry, maintaining an electrical balance that is fundamental to health, performance, and cellular vitality.

## The body's natural electrical balance

The human body maintains its natural electrical balance through the precise regulation of charged particles, or ions, across cellular membranes and within extracellular and intracellular fluids, a dynamic equilibrium essential for nerve conduction, muscle contraction, cardiac rhythm, and metabolic homeostasis. At the foundation of this balance is the resting membrane potential, a voltage difference established primarily by the sodium–potassium ATPase pump, which consumes ATP to export three sodium ions out of cells and import two potassium ions, creating an electrochemical gradient. This gradient underpins the ability of cells to generate rapid electrical signals—action potentials—when voltage-gated ion channels open in response to stimuli, allowing a transient influx of sodium ions that depolarizes the membrane, followed by potassium efflux that repolarizes it and restores the resting state. In neurons, such action potentials propagate along axons to transmit information between the brain, spinal cord, and peripheral organs, while in muscle fibres they trigger calcium release from the sarcoplasmic reticulum, enabling actin–myosin interactions and muscle contraction.

•The heart utilizes specialized pacemaker cells in the sinoatrial node, which possess unstable resting potentials due to "funny" channels permeable to sodium and potassium, to generate rhythmic impulses that spread through the atrioventricular node and Purkinje fibres, orchestrating organized atrial and ventricular contractions. Beyond these rapid electrical events, the body's fluids—including blood plasma and interstitial fluid—serve as conductive media that facilitate the distribution of ions and maintain acid-base equilibrium, regulated by the kidneys through electrolyte reabsorption and excretion, and by the lungs via carbon dioxide and bicarbonate buffering. Hormonal systems, notably the renin–angiotensin–aldosterone axis, further fine-tune sodium and potassium levels, while parathyroid hormone and calcitonin adjust calcium and phosphate concentrations, influencing electrical stability in neurons and myocytes. Membrane potential homeostasis also depends on chloride channels, which stabilize cells by offsetting excessive depolarization, and on gap junctions that enable direct electrical coupling between adjacent cardiomyocytes. At the subcellular level, redox reactions within mitochondria and throughout metabolic pathways involve controlled electron transfers that contribute to the cell's overall charge balance and energy production. When electrolyte imbalances arise—due to dehydration, renal dysfunction, or endocrine disorders—the resulting disturbances in membrane potentials can manifest as muscle weakness, cramps, arrhythmias, or neurological deficits. Adequate hydration and balanced electrolyte intake are crucial to maintain the volume and ionic composition of bodily fluids, ensuring that the electric currents responsible for cellular communication can flow without impedance.

Moreover, insulating structures such as myelin sheaths around neurons and the multi-layered skin protect the body from external electrical disturbances and direct ion currents along designated pathways, preventing random leakage of voltage. Diseases that disrupt ion channel function, known as channelopathies, further highlight the importance of electrical balance, as mutations in sodium, potassium, or calcium channels can lead to epilepsy, cardiac arrhythmias, or muscle disorders. Medical monitoring tools such as electrocardiograms and nerve conduction studies measure the body's electrical activity, providing diagnostic insights into disturbances of this delicate balance. Emerging research into grounding, or earthing, explores whether contact with Earth's surface electrons can influence the body's charge distribution and reduce oxidative stress, though more rigorous studies are required. Ultimately, the human body's natural electrical balance is a testament to evolutionary optimization, whereby complex interactions among ion channels, pumps, hormonal controls, fluid compartments, and redox chemistry sustain the electrical forces that drive life's essential processes.

## The Earth's Electrical Properties

## The Earth's negative charge

The Earth, our home in the cosmos, is not only a marvel of geology, biology, and atmospheric science, but also a fascinating subject within the field of electricity. One lesser-known but fundamental aspect of our planet is its natural negative electric charge. This property plays a crucial role in atmospheric phenomena and even impacts life on the planet's surface.

At its core, the Earth's negative charge stems from the distribution of electrons on and near its surface. The surface of the Earth is rich in free electrons, giving it a net negative charge compared to the atmosphere above. This is not an arbitrary trait, but rather the outcome of various physical processes that have shaped the planet over billions of years.

To understand why the Earth carries a negative charge, we must consider the concept of the Earth as an electrical body in a vast system. The planet and its atmosphere act as a gigantic capacitor—a device used to store electrical energy. The Earth's surface is negatively charged, while the upper atmosphere, particularly the ionosphere (a layer of ionized gases high above the surface), is relatively positive. The difference in charge between the ground and the ionosphere creates what is known as the atmospheric electric field.

This field is maintained and continually replenished through natural processes, most notably thunderstorms. During a thunderstorm, powerful updrafts and collisions of water droplets and ice particles generate separation of electric charges within clouds. The tops of thunderstorm clouds tend to become positively charged, while the bases become negatively charged. As a result, negative charge is delivered from the cloud to the ground, helping sustain the Earth's net negative charge over time.

The Earth's negative charge is not static; it is constantly being lost to the positively charged atmosphere through a gentle flow of electric current known as the "fair weather current." This current is incredibly small—on the order of a few microamperes per square kilometer—but it is continuous. Thunderstorms around the world act as natural "batteries," pumping negative charge back to the Earth's surface and maintaining the global electrical balance.

The presence of the Earth's negative charge also has practical and biological implications. For example, when humans walk across carpets or touch metal objects, they may discharge static electricity to the ground. This is possible because the Earth acts as a vast reservoir, readily accepting extra electrons. In terms of biological effects, some researchers propose that direct physical contact with the Earth—such as walking barefoot, a practice called "earthing"—may have subtle health benefits, potentially due to the transfer of electrons from the ground to the body.

Furthermore, the Earth's negative charge is essential for atmospheric phenomena like lightning. Lightning occurs when the potential difference between clouds and the ground becomes large enough to overcome the insulating properties of air, resulting in a sudden discharge of electricity.

Concluding, the Earth's negative electric charge is a fundamental, yet often overlooked, property that plays a significant role in the planet's electrical environment. It is sustained by complex interactions between the ground and the atmosphere, especially thunderstorms, and has implications for both natural phenomena and daily human life.

Understanding the Earth's negative charge helps us appreciate the dynamic and interconnected nature of our planet.

How does the Earth maintains its electrical state?

The Earth is more than just a physical mass of rock and water; it is an active participant in a vast, dynamic system of electrical activity. The planet maintains a persistent electrical state, characterized by a negatively charged surface and a positively charged atmosphere. This global electrical circuit is not static—it is continually renewed and balanced through a complex interplay of natural processes. Understanding how Earth sustains this electrical equilibrium reveals much about our planet's atmospheric phenomena and the invisible forces shaping our environment.

At the heart of Earth's electrical state is what scientists call the **global atmospheric electric circuit**. This circuit is analogous to a giant battery or capacitor, with the Earth's surface forming one plate (negative) and the ionosphere, a layer of charged particles high in the atmosphere, forming the other (positive). The voltage difference between the Earth and the ionosphere typically measures about 250,000 to 300,000 volts. Maintaining this difference requires constant movement and replenishment of electrical charge.

## Thunderstorms and Lightning: Nature's Generators

The most significant contributors to the Earth's electrical state are thunderstorms and lightning. Within thunderstorm clouds, collisions between ice particles and water droplets cause a separation of electric charges. The upper regions of the storm cloud become positively charged, while the lower regions become negatively charged. This charge separation creates strong electrical fields within the cloud and between the cloud and the ground.

When the potential difference becomes large enough, lightning discharges occur, transferring negative charge from the cloud to the Earth's surface. On a global scale, thousands of thunderstorms are active at any given moment, collectively delivering about 1,000 to 2,000 amperes of current to the Earth's surface. This constant input replenishes the negative charge lost from the ground, helping to maintain the planet's overall electrical state.

## The Fair Weather Current

Even when skies are clear, a subtle electrical process continues. The Earth's negative surface charge is gradually lost to the atmosphere via the "fair weather current." In regions away from thunderstorms, the air conducts a slow upward flow of positive ions, while electrons flow downward toward the surface. This fair weather current is weak—about 2 picoamperes per square meter—but over the entire surface of the planet, it amounts to a significant transfer of charge.

## The Role of the Ionosphere and Cosmic Rays

The ionosphere, a region of the atmosphere ionized by solar ultraviolet radiation and cosmic rays, plays a crucial role. It acts as the upper "plate" of the Earth's capacitor and is highly conductive. Cosmic rays from space and solar radiation continually ionize the atmosphere, enabling it to conduct electricity and allowing the global circuit to function. The movement of charges in thunderstorms, and the fair weather currents, are all possible because the ionosphere and the lower atmosphere maintain their conductivity.

## Human Influence

While natural processes dominate, human activity can influence the Earth's electrical state. Activities like pollution, nuclear tests, and radio transmissions can alter the conductivity of the atmosphere and affect local or regional electrical balances.

In summary, the Earth's electrical state is maintained by a dynamic balance between charge delivered to the surface by thunderstorms and lost via fair weather currents, all operating within the framework of the global atmospheric electric circuit. The planet's ability to sustain this state is a testament to the interconnected and self-regulating systems that make Earth unique in the solar system.

## How the Earth maintains its electrical state

The Earth's electrical state is an elegant and continuous interplay of atmospheric, geological, and cosmic processes. At its core, Earth behaves like a vast electrical sphere, with its surface holding a net negative charge while the upper atmosphere, particularly the ionosphere, is positive. The voltage difference between the ground and the ionosphere hovers around 250,000 to 300,000 volts. This voltage is not a static property but is dynamically maintained through a series of natural mechanisms that constantly move and balance electrical charges between the planet and its surrounding atmosphere.

A primary mechanism behind this persistent electrical state is the global atmospheric electric circuit. This circuit can be conceptualized as a planetary-scale loop where charges are continuously transported and redistributed. Thunderstorms and electrified clouds are fundamental in this process. Inside thunderclouds, collisions between water droplets, ice, and hail create a separation of charges; generally, positive charges accumulate at the top and negative charges at the bottom of the cloud. The base of the cloud, being negatively charged, induces a positive charge on the surface directly below it. When the charge separation becomes sufficiently intense, lightning occurs. Lightning is much more than a dramatic visual event—it is the principal way negative charge is delivered from the atmosphere back down to the Earth's surface.

Globally, at any given moment, there are about 2,000 thunderstorms occurring, producing approximately 40–100 lightning flashes per second. Each lightning strike transfers an immense quantity of electrons, collectively amounting to an average current of around 1,800 amperes distributed globally. This input is crucial because it replenishes the negative surface charge that is constantly being lost to the atmosphere.

Between stormy episodes, the atmosphere is not electrically dormant. In fair weather conditions, there is a steady but minuscule movement of positive ions from the atmosphere down to the Earth's surface, and electrons flow from the surface upward—a phenomenon known as the fair weather current. This current, although very weak (measured in picoamperes per square meter), is continuous and global. It is the quiet counterpart to the dramatic charge transfer of lightning, and it is responsible for the slow but steady leakage of the Earth's negative charge into the atmosphere. As charge is lost, thunderstorms restore it, maintaining overall balance.

The ionosphere plays a vital supporting role. This high-altitude layer, ionized by solar ultraviolet radiation and cosmic rays, is highly conductive and acts as the reservoir of positive charge in the global circuit. Cosmic rays and solar radiation continually ionize atmospheric gases, especially at higher altitudes, ensuring that the air remains conductive enough for the circuit to function. The interplay between the Earth's surface, the conductive atmosphere, and the ionosphere forms a complete electrical "loop" that is constantly energized and maintained.

Even daily and seasonal changes influence this system. For example, the distribution and frequency of thunderstorms shift with weather patterns, seasons, and the solar cycle, subtly altering the global circuit's characteristics. In addition, volcanic eruptions, cosmic events, and even human activities (such as pollution or nuclear explosions) can temporarily affect atmospheric conductivity and the behaviour of the circuit.

Through these interconnected processes—storm-driven charge separation and delivery, steady fair weather current, and continuous ionization by solar and cosmic radiation—the Earth sustains its unique and delicate electrical state. This system is a testament to the dynamic, self-regulating mechanisms that pervade our planet's atmosphere and environment.

The electric field between the Earth's surface and the atmosphere is a remarkable and persistent feature of our planet's electrical environment. This field, typically measuring around 100 volts per meter at ground level in fair weather, is directed downward, indicating that the Earth is negatively charged relative to the atmosphere above. The maintenance of this electric field is the result of a dynamic and global interplay among atmospheric processes, weather phenomena, and cosmic influences.

## The electric field between the Earth and atmosphere

At the heart of this phenomenon lies the **global atmospheric electric circuit**. This circuit functions much like an immense, natural battery, with the Earth's surface acting as the negative terminal and the ionosphere, a region of charged particles high in the atmosphere, serving as the positive terminal. The voltage difference between these two "plates" can reach several hundred thousand volts. For the field to remain stable, there must be a continuous supply and redistribution of electric charges—a process sustained primarily by thunderstorms and electrified clouds.

Thunderstorms are the primary generators in this circuit. Inside a thunderstorm, complex interactions among rising air currents, water droplets, and ice particles cause a separation of electrical charges. Typically, the upper parts of the cloud become positively charged, while the lower regions accumulate a negative charge. When the charge separation becomes great enough, it leads to lightning—a spectacular transfer of electrons from clouds to the Earth's surface. This process delivers negative charge to the ground, reinforcing the Earth's negative potential relative to the atmosphere.

At any given time, there are about 2,000 thunderstorms occurring worldwide, producing approximately 40 to 100 lightning flashes every second. Each flash transfers a substantial amount of charge, and the combined effect is a global current of about 1,800 amperes. This constant input is crucial; without it, the Earth would gradually lose its negative charge, and the electric field between the surface and the atmosphere would diminish.

However, loss of charge is an ongoing process as well. In regions where the weather is clear and calm—so-called fair weather regions — the electric field drives a continuous, though tiny, current of positive ions from the atmosphere down to the Earth, and electrons from the Earth upward. This "fair weather current" is estimated to be about 2 picoamperes per square meter, but when multiplied over the surface of the Earth, it represents a significant flow of charge. Thus, the fair weather current gradually neutralizes the Earth's negative charge, necessitating replenishment by thunderstorms.

The ionosphere plays a critical role in this system. Maintained by solar ultraviolet radiation and cosmic rays, the ionosphere is highly conductive and acts as a vast reservoir of positive charge. Its conductivity ensures that the upper end of the electric field remains stable and allows charges to travel freely within the global circuit.

Cosmic rays and solar radiation also contribute by continually ionizing atmospheric molecules, especially in the upper atmosphere, which keeps the entire atmospheric column conductive enough for the electric field and current to persist.

This delicate balance—charges supplied by storms and lost via fair weather currents, with the ionosphere as a positive terminal—keeps the electric field between the Earth and atmosphere alive. It is a subtle, invisible force, yet it is essential for phenomena ranging from lightning to the behaviour of atmospheric ions, and it underscores the dynamic nature of Earth's environment.

# How Earthing Works

## Earthing Explained: A Beginner's Guide to Grounding and Its Benefits

### How Earthing / Grounding Works: The Basics

Earthing, also known as grounding, is a concept rooted in both electrical engineering and holistic health. At its core, earthing refers to the direct physical contact between the human body and the Earth's surface, such as walking barefoot on grass, soil, or sand, or using conductive systems that connect indoors to the ground outside. While the term is often associated with wellness practices, it is fundamentally based on the principles of electricity and the Earth's natural electric charge.

In electrical engineering, grounding is a safety technique that involves connecting electrical circuits to the Earth. This connection provides a pathway for excess or stray electrical charge (often from a fault or lightning strike) to safely dissipate into the ground. The Earth acts as a massive reservoir of electrons, capable of absorbing or supplying electrons as needed to maintain electrical neutrality. Grounding prevents electrical shocks, protects equipment, and helps stabilize voltage levels in power systems.

The biological aspect of earthing is inspired by this same property of the Earth as an electron-rich environment. The surface of the Earth carries a negative charge due to a surplus of free electrons. This charge is maintained by global atmospheric processes such as thunderstorms, which deliver electrons to the ground. When a person comes into direct contact with the Earth, or connects to it via a conductive wire, their body can absorb some of these electrons, equalizing their electrical potential with that of the Earth.

The human body is conductive, largely due to its water and mineral content. In modern life, people often wear shoes with insulating soles and spend most of their time indoors, isolated from the Earth's surface. This isolation can allow the body to accumulate static charges or be exposed to electromagnetic fields (EMFs) from electronic devices. Direct contact with the Earth provides a way for excess charge to be neutralized. If the body has a positive charge, electrons from the Earth flow into it; if the body is negatively charged, electrons may flow out. This process is automatic and governed by the principle that charge moves to equalize differences in electrical potential.

## Earthing Explained: A Beginner's Guide to Grounding and Its Benefits

Research into the health effects of earthing is ongoing, but some studies suggest that grounding may reduce inflammation, improve sleep, and lower stress by stabilizing the body's electrical environment. The proposed mechanism centres on the flow of electrons from the Earth into the body, which may help neutralize free radicals, molecules that contribute to oxidative stress and inflammation. Other potential benefits include reduced pain and improved circulation, although more robust scientific evidence is needed to confirm these effects.

Earthing can be practised in simple ways—walking barefoot on natural surfaces, gardening with bare hands, or swimming in natural bodies of water. There are also products such as grounding mats or sheets that connect to the Earth via a wire and can be used indoors, though these should be used with proper guidance to ensure safety.

Earthing or grounding works by taking advantage of the Earth's vast store of free electrons. By allowing the human body to exchange electrons with the ground, this practice helps neutralize electrical imbalances and may contribute to overall health and well-being. The process is a blend of ancient wisdom and modern science, rooted in the fundamental laws of electricity that govern our planet.

## The Process of Grounding via Barefoot Walking or Using Conductive Materials

Grounding, also known as earthing, is the practice of physically connecting the human body to the Earth's surface, either by walking barefoot outdoors or by using specially designed conductive materials indoors. This process is grounded in the principles of physics, biology, and—more recently—wellness science. The fundamental idea is that direct contact with the Earth allows for the transfer of electrons between the body and the ground, which can neutralize electrical imbalances and potentially promote health.

The Earth's surface carries a natural negative electric charge, maintained by global atmospheric phenomena such as thunderstorms. This charge is characterized by a vast reserve of free electrons. The human body, being composed largely of water and minerals, is a good conductor of electricity. In our daily lives, however, we are often insulated from the Earth by shoes with rubber or plastic soles, buildings with synthetic flooring, and time spent in vehicles. These insulators prevent the body from naturally discharging accumulated static electricity or from equilibrating its electrical potential with that of the Earth.

## Barefoot Walking

One of the simplest and most effective ways to ground the body is by walking barefoot on natural surfaces like grass, soil, sand, or stone. When the soles of the feet make direct contact with the Earth, the skin creates a conductive bridge, allowing electrons to flow freely. If the body has a positive electric charge (an excess of protons or a deficit of electrons), electrons from the ground move into the body to neutralize this imbalance. Conversely, if the body has a surplus of electrons, they can flow out to the Earth, which acts as an infinite sink or source for electrical charge. The process is automatic and governed by the principle that electrical charge moves to equalize potential differences.

The act of grounding through barefoot walking is not only immediate but also continuous as long as the skin remains in contact with the Earth. The rate of electron transfer can be influenced by the moisture and mineral content of the ground, as wet or mineral-rich soil is more conductive than dry, sandy, or rocky surfaces.

## Using Conductive Materials

For those who cannot regularly spend time outdoors, grounding can also be achieved indoors through the use of conductive materials. These include grounding mats, sheets, wristbands, or patches made with conductive fibers such as silver or carbon. Such products are connected via a wire to a grounding rod inserted into the Earth outside, or plugged into the grounding port of a properly wired electrical outlet (which is ultimately connected to the Earth through a building's electrical system).

When a person touches or lies on these conductive products, the pathway allows electrons to flow between the body and the Earth, mimicking the effects of direct outdoor contact. It is crucial that these materials are properly designed and safely installed to prevent exposure to electrical faults. When used correctly, these devices offer a practical solution for grounding in modern, indoor environments.

# Earthing Explained: A Beginner's Guide to Grounding and Its Benefits

## Physiological Implications

Scientific studies, though limited, suggest possible health benefits to grounding, such as reduced inflammation, improved sleep, and decreased stress, potentially due to the neutralization of free radicals in the body. The mechanism is believed to involve the transfer of electrons, which may act as antioxidants and stabilize the body's electrical environment.

In essence, grounding via barefoot walking or conductive materials harnesses the Earth's natural energy, providing a simple yet profound way for the body to maintain electrical balance in an increasingly insulated world.

## Transfer of Electrons from the Earth to the Body during Earthing / Grounding

As stated previously, Earthing, also known as grounding, is the practice of making direct physical contact with the Earth's surface, typically by walking barefoot on grass, soil, or sand, or by using conductive materials that connect the body to the ground. While this practice has ancient roots in human history, its mechanisms are now being explored through the lens of modern science. At the core of earthing lies the transfer of electrons from the Earth to the human body—a process with profound implications for our electrical state and potentially our health.

The Earth behaves as an enormous reservoir of free electrons, continuously replenished by global atmospheric phenomena such as thunderstorms and lightning strikes. These processes maintain a net negative charge at the planet's surface. In contrast, modern living often insulates us from this reservoir. Shoes with rubber or synthetic soles, buildings elevated above the ground, and extended time spent indoors all prevent direct electrical contact with the Earth. As a result, the human body can become electrically imbalanced, accumulating static charges or being exposed to electromagnetic fields from electronic devices.

When a person practices earthing, such as by walking barefoot on moist grass or soil, a conductive bridge is formed between the body and the Earth. The skin, rich in sweat and electrolytes, is a reasonable conductor, especially when in contact with moist surfaces. Through this connection, electrons—negatively charged particles—can flow freely from the Earth into the body. The direction and magnitude of this electron flow are governed by the principle of electrical potential: electrons move from areas of higher concentration (the Earth) to areas of lower concentration (a positively charged or neutral body) until equilibrium is achieved.

This transfer of electrons is not merely theoretical; it can be measured with sensitive instruments. Studies have shown that when individuals are grounded, their bodies quickly equalize to the same electrical potential as the Earth. In practical terms, this means that any excess positive charge in the body is neutralized as electrons from the ground flow in, helping to stabilize the body's electrical environment.

The physiological implications of this electron transfer are a subject of growing scientific interest. One leading hypothesis centers on the role of electrons as natural antioxidants. Free radicals—unstable molecules with unpaired electrons—are produced in the body through normal metabolism and in response to stress or injury. These free radicals can damage cells and tissues in a process known as oxidative stress, which is linked to inflammation and various chronic diseases. It is proposed that electrons absorbed from the Earth can neutralize free radicals by pairing with their unpaired electrons, thus reducing oxidative stress and inflammation.

Emerging research suggests that grounding may result in measurable biological effects, including reduced markers of inflammation, improved blood flow, and changes in stress hormone levels. Participants in grounding studies have reported improved sleep, faster recovery from exercise, and reduced pain, though more rigorous research is needed to fully understand these benefits.

The the transfer of electrons from the Earth to the body during earthing or grounding is a fundamental process rooted in the laws of physics and electricity. By reconnecting with the Earth's natural supply of electrons, individuals may help restore electrical balance in their bodies, potentially influencing physiological processes and overall well-being. This age-old practice, now supported by emerging scientific evidence, highlights the subtle yet significant ways in which we are connected to the planet beneath our feet.

## The role of skin contact and conductivity

The role of skin contact and conductivity is fundamental to many physiological and technological processes, influencing everything from how our bodies interact with the environment to the effectiveness of medical devices and electrical systems. Skin, the largest organ in the human body, serves as the primary interface between our internal systems and the outside world. Its ability to conduct electricity depends on numerous factors, including its structure, composition, moisture content, and the presence of electrolytes.

Human skin comprises several layers, with the outermost being the stratum corneum. This layer consists of dead, flattened cells and serves as a barrier, protecting underlying tissues from pathogens, chemicals, and physical damage. While the stratum corneum is a relatively poor conductor of electricity when dry, its conductive properties change dramatically with hydration. The presence of sweat, which contains water and dissolved electrolytes such as sodium, potassium, and chloride ions, significantly increases the skin's conductivity. These ions facilitate the flow of electric current across the skin, transforming it from a natural insulator to a competent conductor.

Conductivity through the skin is also influenced by the thickness of the stratum corneum. Areas with thinner skin, such as the inner arms or the face, offer less resistance to electrical flow than areas with thicker skin, like the soles of the feet or palms. Moreover, any cuts, abrasions, or disruptions to the skin barrier further increase conductivity by exposing underlying, more conductive tissues.

Temperature plays an integral role as well. Warm temperatures stimulate sweat glands, leading to increased moisture and ion content on the skin's surface, thus lowering electrical resistance. Conversely, cold conditions reduce sweat production, dry the skin, and diminish conductivity. This explains why devices that rely on skin contact, such as biometric sensors, sometimes perform less effectively in dry or cold environments.

# Earthing Explained: A Beginner's Guide to Grounding and Its Benefits

The significance of skin contact and conductivity extends deeply into medical and technological fields. Electrocardiograms (ECGs), electroencephalograms (EEGs), and other biosensors depend on the ability to detect tiny electrical signals generated by the body. To enhance conductivity and ensure accurate readings, conductive gels or adhesives are often applied to the skin, minimizing resistance and improving signal transmission. Similarly, in defibrillation or transcutaneous electrical nerve stimulation (TENS), ensuring good skin contact with conductive pads is essential for effective energy transfer and patient safety.

In the context of safety, the skin's conductivity is a double-edged sword. While it allows for beneficial diagnostic and therapeutic applications, it also means the body is susceptible to harm from external electrical currents. The degree of risk depends on the path the current takes, its strength, and the condition of the skin. Dry, intact skin offers some protection, but when wet or broken, the body becomes more vulnerable to electric shock.

Beyond technology, skin conductivity has been used as a physiological marker in research. Galvanic skin response (GSR)—the measurement of skin's electrical conductance—serves as an indicator of psychological or emotional arousal, used in lie detection and stress studies.

In summary, skin contact and conductivity are pivotal in mediating interactions between the body and external electrical sources. The skin's structure, moisture, temperature, and integrity collectively determine its conductive properties, shaping the outcomes in both health-related and technological applications. Understanding these factors is essential for optimizing safety, enhancing device performance, and interpreting physiological signals.

## Free Radicals and Oxidative Stress

## What are free radicals?

What Are Free Radicals in Our Body? What Do They Do?

Free radicals are unstable molecules that play a significant role in various biological processes within our bodies. To understand free radicals, it helps to remember a basic principle of chemistry: atoms and molecules are most stable when their outermost shells are filled with electrons. Normally, atoms have paired electrons, but a free radical is a molecule or atom that has an unpaired electron in its outer shell. This unpaired electron makes free radicals highly reactive and unstable.

### How Are Free Radicals Formed?

In the human body, free radicals are formed naturally as byproducts of normal metabolic processes. For example, when our cells generate energy from food via cellular respiration, small amounts of free radicals are produced. Additionally, our immune system uses free radicals to help destroy bacteria and viruses during an immune response.

However, free radicals can also be generated from external sources, such as:

- Pollution

- Cigarette smoke

- Radiation (including UV light from the sun)

- Certain chemicals and toxins

- Some medications

### What Do Free Radicals Do in the Body?

Because of their unpaired electron, free radicals seek out other molecules from which they can "steal" an electron to achieve stability. This process is called oxidation. When free radicals interact with other molecules in the body—such as DNA, proteins, or cell membranes—they can cause damage by altering their structure and function. This chain reaction of damage is known as oxidative stress.

Consequences of Free Radical Activity

Oxidative stress and the resulting damage can contribute to aging and to the development of various diseases, including:

- **Cancer**: Free radicals can damage DNA, potentially causing mutations that contribute to cancer development.

- **Cardiovascular disease**: Oxidative damage to cholesterol and blood vessel walls is linked to the development of atherosclerosis (hardening of the arteries).

- **Neurodegenerative diseases**: Conditions like Alzheimer's and Parkinson's diseases have been associated with oxidative damage to brain cells.

- **Inflammation and immune dysfunction**: Chronic oxidative stress can disrupt normal immune responses and promote inflammation.

**Are Free Radicals Always Bad?**

Despite their reputation, free radicals are not always harmful. In fact, some free radicals are necessary for life. The immune system, for instance, uses free radicals to attack and destroy invading pathogens. Additionally, free radicals play roles in cell signalling and other essential biological processes.

Problems arise when there is an imbalance—when the body produces more free radicals than it can neutralize. This imbalance leads to oxidative stress.

**How Does the Body Defend Itself?**

To combat the potentially damaging effects of free radicals, the body has evolved a complex system of antioxidants. Antioxidants are molecules that can safely donate an electron to a free radical, neutralizing it without becoming unstable themselves. The body produces some antioxidants naturally (like glutathione), and others are obtained from the diet (such as vitamins C and E, and plant compounds like flavonoids).

**Summary**

In summary, free radicals are unstable molecules with unpaired electrons produced both naturally in the body and from environmental sources. While they play important roles in health, excessive free radical activity leads to oxidative stress, which can damage cells and contribute to aging and disease. Antioxidants are the body's defense mechanism, helping to maintain the balance and protect against free radical-induced damage.

## How free radicals affect health

Free radicals are highly reactive molecules with unpaired electrons, and their impact on human health is profound and wide-ranging. Though a natural by-product of normal processes like metabolism and immune defence, free radicals can cause significant harm when present in excess —a situation known as oxidative stress. The effects of free radicals on health span from the aging process to the development of chronic diseases, making their management critically important for well-being.

## Cellular and Molecular Damage

The primary danger of free radicals lies in their ability to damage important cellular components such as DNA, proteins, and lipids (fats). Because free radicals are unstable, they seek to stabilize themselves by reacting with nearby molecules, often "stealing" electrons. This initiates chain reactions that can alter the structure and function of vital molecules. For instance, when free radicals attack the fatty acids in cell membranes, they cause lipid peroxidation, which disrupts cell integrity and can lead to cell death. Similarly, free radical-induced damage to DNA can result in mutations that disrupt normal cell function or trigger the uncontrolled cell growth seen in cancer.

## Ageing and Degeneration

One of the most widely accepted theories of ageing is the "free radical theory of ageing." Over time, accumulated oxidative damage from free radicals impairs cell function and tissue structure, leading to the gradual decline associated with ageing. Observable signs of this process include wrinkles, loss of skin elasticity, and diminished organ function. On a deeper level, the brain and nervous system are particularly vulnerable due to their high oxygen consumption and lipid-rich composition, contributing to age-related neurodegenerative diseases.

## Chronic Diseases

Oxidative stress is involved in the development and progression of numerous chronic diseases:

Cardiovascular Disease: Free radicals contribute to the oxidation of low-density lipoprotein (LDL) cholesterol in the blood. Oxidized LDL is more likely to accumulate in artery walls, leading to atherosclerosis (hardening and narrowing of arteries), which increases the risk of heart attacks and strokes.

Cancer: DNA damage caused by free radicals can result in mutations that disrupt normal cell regulation. Over time, these mutations can accumulate and lead to the uncontrolled cell division that characterizes cancer.

Neurodegenerative Diseases: Disorders such as Alzheimer's and Parkinson's diseases are linked to oxidative stress in brain cells. Free radical damage impairs neuron function and promotes the buildup of toxic proteins, contributing to cognitive decline and movement disorders.

Inflammatory Conditions: Oxidative stress can trigger chronic inflammation, which is a common underlying factor in diseases like rheumatoid arthritis, diabetes, and inflammatory bowel disease.

•

## Immune System Effects

While the immune system uses free radicals to destroy pathogens, excessive free radicals can weaken immune defenses. Chronic oxidative stress impairs the ability of immune cells to function properly, making the body more susceptible to infections and slowing recovery from illness.

## Prevention and Balance

The body has natural antioxidant defences to counteract free radicals, and a diet rich in antioxidants (found in fruits, vegetables, nuts, and whole grains) helps maintain this balance. However, lifestyle factors such as smoking, excessive alcohol consumption, exposure to pollution, and poor diet can overwhelm these defences, increasing disease risk.

Concluding: Free radicals, while necessary for some physiological processes, can have detrimental effects on health when not kept in check. Their ability to damage cells and tissues underlies ageing and the development of many chronic diseases. Supporting the body's antioxidant defences through healthy living is key to reducing the harmful impacts of free radicals.

## The concept of electron donation and neutralization

The Concept of Electron Donation and Neutralization in the Body: Our bodies are constantly engaged in complex chemical processes that keep us alive and healthy. Among these, the concept of electron donation and neutralization is especially important for protecting cells from damage and maintaining overall health. This concept is most commonly illustrated in the context of free radicals and antioxidants.

## What Is Electron Donation?

At the atomic level, electrons are tiny, negatively charged particles that orbit the nucleus of an atom. Atoms and molecules are most stable when their electrons are paired. Sometimes, however, chemical reactions in the body produce molecules known as free radicals—atoms or molecules that have an unpaired electron. Because of this unpaired electron, free radicals are highly reactive. They seek to achieve stability by "stealing" an electron from a neighbouring molecule, a process called oxidation.

## The Problem with Free Radicals

When a free radical steals an electron from another molecule (such as DNA, proteins, or cell membrane lipids), it causes damage to that molecule, turning it into a new free radical. This can set off a chain reaction, leading to widespread cellular damage. Over time, this oxidative damage contributes to aging, inflammation, and diseases such as cancer and cardiovascular disease.

## Role of Antioxidants: Electron Donation as Defence

The body has a built-in defence system to counteract free radicals, and this is where electron donation comes into play. Molecules known as antioxidants can safely donate an electron to a free radical without becoming unstable themselves. By donating an electron, antioxidants neutralize free radicals, stopping the chain reaction of damage.

For example, vitamin C (ascorbic acid) is a powerful antioxidant. When it encounters a free radical, vitamin C donates one of its electrons to the unstable molecule. This donation stabilizes the free radical, preventing it from causing further harm. Importantly, vitamin C remains stable even after losing an electron, meaning it does not become a free radical itself.

43

## How the Body Maintains Balance

The body produces its own antioxidants, such as glutathione, superoxide dismutase, and catalase. Additionally, many antioxidants are obtained from the diet (e.g., vitamins C and E, selenium, and plant phytochemicals like flavonoids and carotenoids). These molecules patrol our cells, constantly neutralizing free radicals by donating electrons.

This balance between free radicals and antioxidants is critical. When the production of free radicals overwhelms antioxidant defenses, oxidative stress occurs, leading to cellular and tissue damage. Conversely, if antioxidant levels are sufficient, they keep free radicals in check, preserving cell health and function.

## Why Is Electron Donation Important?

Electron donation is essential to life because it prevents the destructive activity of free radicals. It protects DNA from mutations, preserves the integrity of cell membranes, and ensures that proteins function correctly. By neutralizing harmful molecules, electron donation by antioxidants supports immune function, slows aging, and reduces the risk of chronic diseases.

Electron donation and neutralization are fundamental chemical processes that protect our bodies from oxidative damage. Antioxidants, by safely donating electrons, neutralize free radicals and stop harmful chain reactions. Maintaining this balance—through the body's own defenses and a diet rich in antioxidants—is key to protecting cells and supporting long-term health.

# The Science Behind Earthing

## Research studies and scientific evidence

Scientific Research on Earthing / Grounding

As previously stated, Earthing** or **grounding** refers to direct physical contact with the Earth's surface electrons, usually by walking barefoot outside or using conductive systems indoors. Proponents claim it reduces inflammation, improves sleep, relieves pain, and enhances well-being. The scientific community has started investigating these claims, though the field is still emerging.

## Mechanism Hypothesis

The main hypothesis is that the Earth's surface has a negative electrical potential, and direct contact allows the body to absorb free electrons, which act as antioxidants. This, in theory, could neutralize free radicals and reduce inflammation and oxidative stress.

## Summary of Key Research Findings

Pain, Inflammation, and Immune Response

Chevalier, G., Sinatra, S. T., Oschman, J. L., Delany, R. M., & Brown, R. (2013).

1). Earthing: Health Implications of Reconnecting the Human Body to the Earth's Surface Electrons. Journal of Environmental and Public Health, 2012, Article ID 291541.

Findings: This review consolidates several studies, concluding that earthing reduces pain, alters blood markers of inflammation, and improves immune response.

2). Blood Viscosity and Cardiovascular Health

Chevalier, G., Sinatra, S. T., & Oschman, J. L. (2013).

Earthing (Grounding) the Human Body Reduces Blood Viscosity—a Major Factor in Cardiovascular Disease. Journal of Alternative and Complementary Medicine, 19(2), 102-110.

Findings: Grounding for two hours significantly reduced blood viscosity in healthy adults, suggesting cardiovascular benefits.

Sleep and Cortisol Rhythm

3). Ghaly, M., & Teplitz, D. (2004).

The Biologic Effects of Grounding the Human Body During Sleep as Measured by Cortisol Levels and Subjective Reporting of Sleep, Pain, and Stress. Journal of Alternative and Complementary Medicine, 10(5), 767-776.

Findings: Grounding during sleep improved cortisol rhythms, sleep quality, and reduced pain and stress.

4). Inflammation and Wound Healing

Brown, D., Chevalier, G., & Hill, M. (2010).

Pilot Study on the Effect of Grounding on Delayed-Onset Muscle Soreness. Journal of Alternative and Complementary Medicine, 16(3), 265-273.

Findings: Subjects who were grounded after exercise experienced less muscle soreness and faster recovery.

•

5). Heart Rate Variability and Stress**

Chevalier, G., & Sinatra, S. T. (2011).

Emotional Stress, Heart Rate Variability, Grounding, and Improved Autonomic Tone: Clinical Applications.

Findings: Grounding increased heart rate variability (a marker of reduced stress and better autonomic function).

6). Electrolytes and Red Blood Cell Charge

Sokal, K., & Sokal, P. (2011).

Earthing the Human Organism Influences Blood Chemistry Markers of Muscle Damage. European Journal of Integrative Medicine, 3(4), e245-e254.

Findings: Grounding reduced blood levels of creatine kinase and other markers of muscle damage after exercise.

7). Mood and Well-being

Chevalier, G. (2015).

The Effects of Grounding (Earthing) on Inflammation, the Immune Response, Wound Healing, and Prevention and Treatment of Chronic Inflammatory and Autoimmune Diseases. Journal of Inflammation Research, 8, 83-96.

Findings: Review of clinical studies suggests grounding may improve mood and overall well-being.

8). Electroencephalograms (EEG) and Brain Function

Oschman, J. L. (2007).

Can Electrons Act as Antioxidants? A Review and Commentary. Journal of Alternative and Complementary Medicine, 13(9), 955-967.

Findings: Review discusses EEG changes and reduced stress after grounding, hinting at changes in brain activity.

9). Balance and Physical Function in Older Adults

Karakas, S., et al. (2015).

The Effects of Earthing on Human Physiology: A Randomized, Double-Blind, Pilot Study. European Review for Medical and Pharmacological Sciences, 19(17), 3238-3244.

Findings: Elderly participants showed improved balance and physical function after grounding sessions.

10). Inflammatory Markers and Immune Function

Menigoz, W., Latz, T. T., Ely, R. A., Kamei, C., & Oschman, J. L. (2019).

Integrative and Lifestyle Medicine Strategies Should Include Earthing (Grounding): Review of Research Evidence and Clinical Observations. EXPLORE: The Journal of Science and Healing, 15(5), 283-290.

Findings: Review of clinical and observational studies highlighting reduced inflammatory markers and improved immune function in grounded subjects.

Critical View & Limitations

Most studies are small-scale, with limited sample sizes and sometimes lacking rigorous double-blind controls.

The physiological mechanisms—while plausible—are still being debated and require further research.

Placebo effects and subjective outcomes (e.g., pain, mood) are difficult to rule out in some studies.

Conclusion of research

Early research and pilot studies suggest that earthing/grounding may have beneficial effects on inflammation, pain, sleep, cardiovascular health, and stress response. However, more robust, large-scale, double-blind research is needed to confirm these effects and fully understand the mechanisms involved. The majority of findings so far are promising but preliminary.

References:

Chevalier G, Sinatra ST, Oschman JL, et al. Earthing: Health Implications of Reconnecting the Human Body to the Earth's Surface Electrons. J Environ Public Health. 2012;2012:291541.

Ghaly M, Teplitz D, 2004. The Biologic Effects of Grounding the Human Body During Sleep. J Altern Complement Med.

Sokal K, Sokal P. Earthing the Human Organism Influences Blood Chemistry Markers. Eur J Integr Med.

Chevalier G, et al. Earthing (Grounding) the Human Body Reduces Blood Viscosity. J Altern Complement Med.

Brown D, Chevalier G, Hill M. Pilot Study on the Effect of Grounding on Delayed-Onset Muscle Soreness. J Altern Complement Med, 2010.

Menigoz W, et al. Integrative and Lifestyle Medicine Strategies Should Include Earthing. Explore.

## How electrons may reduce inflammation and oxidative damage

How Electrons May Reduce Inflammation and Oxidative Damage in the Body: Inflammation and oxidative damage are central to the development and progression of many chronic diseases, including cardiovascular disease, diabetes, arthritis, and neurodegenerative disorders. In recent years, scientists have explored the role of electrons—particularly those obtained from the Earth through grounding or earthing—in reducing both inflammation and oxidative damage in the human body. Understanding how electrons interact with biological processes offers fascinating insights into potential natural strategies for supporting health.

### The Science of Oxidative Stress

Oxidative stress occurs when there is an imbalance between the production of **free radicals** (unstable molecules with unpaired electrons) and the body's ability to neutralize them with **antioxidants**. Free radicals are a normal by-product of metabolism and immune responses, but in excess, they can damage DNA, proteins, and cell membranes. This damage triggers and perpetuates inflammation—a process by which the body attempts to heal itself but, if chronic, can lead to tissue destruction and disease.

## Electrons as Antioxidants

Electrons play a crucial role in neutralizing free radicals. Antioxidants work by donating electrons to free radicals, stabilizing them and halting the chain reactions that cause cellular damage. Traditionally, antioxidants are obtained from the diet—such as vitamin C, vitamin E, and plant phytochemicals. However, research suggests that the Earth itself is a vast reservoir of free electrons. When the human body comes into direct contact with the Earth (e.g., walking barefoot or using grounding devices), it may absorb some of these electrons.

## Grounding and Electron Transfer

The **grounding** or **earthing** hypothesis proposes that direct physical contact with the Earth allows electrons to flow into the body, where they can act as nature's most abundant antioxidants. These free electrons are thought to migrate to sites of inflammation and oxidative stress, where they neutralize excess free radicals. This process may reduce the inflammatory response and help protect tissues from damage.

## Evidence from Research

Several studies support the idea that electron transfer from the Earth may reduce inflammation and oxidative stress. For example, a study published in the *Journal of Inflammation Research* (Chevalier et al., 2015) found that grounding reduced blood markers of inflammation and improved recovery from muscle soreness after exercise. Other research has shown that grounded subjects had lower levels of white blood cell counts and cytokines, both of which are indicators of inflammation.

-

Additionally, studies have reported that earthing can reduce blood viscosity—a risk factor for cardiovascular disease—by improving the electrical charge on red blood cells, thus preventing clumping and improving circulation. These findings suggest that electrons from the Earth may have a protective effect on the cardiovascular system by reducing inflammation and oxidative damage.

## Mechanisms of Action

The precise mechanisms by which electrons reduce inflammation involve neutralizing reactive oxygen species (ROS)—a type of free radical generated during cellular metabolism and especially during immune responses. When electrons are available, they can pair with the unpaired electrons of ROS, rendering them harmless. This prevents the cascade of oxidative damage and interrupts the cycle of chronic inflammation.

Electrons, whether obtained from dietary antioxidants or potentially absorbed from the Earth through grounding, have the ability to neutralize free radicals and reduce oxidative stress. By donating electrons, these natural antioxidants help to control inflammation, protect tissues from damage, and support overall health. While more research is needed, especially in large-scale human trials, the concept of electrons as powerful allies against inflammation and oxidative damage is gaining scientific support and holds promise for natural, accessible health interventions.

## The connection between grounding and improved health

Over the past two decades, a growing body of scientific research has suggested that grounding may be linked to a variety of health benefits, ranging from reduced inflammation and pain to improved sleep and mood. Here's how grounding is thought to connect to improved health:

## Earthing Explained: A Beginner's Guide to Grounding and Its Benefits

### 1. Electrical Balance and Free Electrons

The Earth's surface carries a subtle negative charge, largely due to its vast store of free electrons. The human body, through daily activities and especially in modern environments, can accumulate positive charges or become electrically imbalanced. Grounding allows the body to absorb electrons from the Earth, helping to restore its natural electrical state. These electrons are believed to act as antioxidants, neutralizing harmful free radicals that cause oxidative stress and inflammation.

### 2. Reduction of Inflammation and Pain

Inflammation is the body's natural response to injury or infection, but chronic inflammation is a root cause of many diseases. Research indicates that grounding can reduce markers of inflammation and pain. For example, studies have shown that people who are grounded after exercise experience less muscle soreness and faster recovery. This effect is thought to occur because the influx of electrons from the Earth neutralizes reactive oxygen species (ROS) and reduces the chain reactions that cause tissue damage and prolonged inflammation.

### 3. Improved Sleep and Stress Reduction

Grounding appears to regulate cortisol, the body's main stress hormone, which influences the sleep-wake cycle. In one landmark study, participants who slept while grounded showed normalized cortisol levels and reported better sleep quality, less stress, and improved mood. The stabilization of the body's internal electrical environment may calm the nervous system and promote better rest.

4. Cardiovascular and Circulatory Benefits

Some research has found that grounding can reduce blood viscosity (thickness), which is a risk factor for cardiovascular disease. By improving the surface charge of red blood cells, grounding may help the blood flow more freely, reducing clot formation and supporting overall heart health. Better circulation also helps deliver nutrients and oxygen to tissues, supporting healing and energy.

5. Support for the Immune System

Since inflammation and immune function are closely linked, grounding's anti-inflammatory effects may also enhance immune system performance. Lower levels of inflammation mean the immune system can function more efficiently, potentially reducing the frequency and severity of infections and autoimmune responses.

6. Mood and Mental Health

Grounding has been associated with improved mood, reduced anxiety, and increased feelings of well-being. This may be due in part to physiological changes (like lower inflammation and pain), as well as the calming effects of direct contact with nature, which is itself known to benefit mental health.

While more large-scale clinical research is needed, current evidence suggests a compelling connection between grounding and improved health. By allowing the body to absorb the Earth's electrons, grounding may help neutralize free radicals, reduce inflammation and pain, improve sleep, support cardiovascular health, and enhance overall well-being. Grounding is a simple, natural practice that may provide meaningful health benefits for many people.

# Practical Ways to Practice Earthing

## Walking barefoot safely

One of the most accessible and popular ways to practice earthing is by walking barefoot outdoors. This simple activity allows the body to connect with the Earth's natural electric charge, which some research suggests may help neutralize free radicals, reduce inflammation, and support overall well-being. However, while walking barefoot can be invigorating and healthful, it is important to consider a variety of safety aspects to ensure the experience remains beneficial and risk-free.

1. Environmental Awareness

Before walking barefoot outdoors, it is crucial to assess the environment for potential hazards. Natural surfaces can harbour sharp objects like broken glass, nails, thorns, or jagged rocks that can puncture or cut the skin. Urban parks, beaches, and trails may look clean but can still conceal hidden dangers. Always scan the area carefully before stepping out of shoes, especially if you are in a location you have not visited barefoot before.

2. Risk of Infections and Parasites

Barefoot walking increases the risk of exposure to infectious agents. Soil in some areas may contain harmful bacteria, fungi, or parasites, such as hookworms, which can enter through broken skin. Animal droppings can also harbour pathogens. After walking barefoot, thoroughly wash your feet with soap and water, especially before touching food or your face. In tropical or subtropical regions, be aware of specific local risks, such as sand fleas or parasites common in the soil.

-

## 3. Allergies and Skin Sensitivities

Some individuals have skin sensitivities or allergies to plants like poison ivy, poison oak, or certain grasses. Direct contact with these plants can cause rashes, itching, or blistering. Learn to identify hazardous plants in your area and avoid walking barefoot where they may grow. If you have a history of skin allergies or eczema, monitor your feet for signs of irritation after earthing sessions.

## 4. Temperature Extremes

The temperature of natural surfaces can vary widely. Hot sand, sun-baked rocks, or cold surfaces can cause burns or discomfort. Always test the ground with your hand or a quick touch of your foot before committing to a longer walk. In cold weather, limit barefoot exposure to avoid frostbite or cold injuries.

## 5. Pre-existing Foot Conditions

People with diabetes, neuropathy, or poor circulation in their feet should be especially cautious. Diminished sensation can make it difficult to notice cuts, blisters, or injuries, which can become infected or lead to serious complications. If you have any medical condition affecting the feet, consult your healthcare provider before practising barefoot earthing.

## 6. Wildlife and Insects

Pay attention to the presence of wildlife such as bees, ants, spiders, or even snakes that can be hidden in grass or leaf litter. In some regions, ticks may also be a concern, particularly in wooded or grassy areas, as they can transmit Lyme disease and other illnesses. Inspect your feet and ankles after each session.

7. Gradual Adaptation**

If you are new to walking barefoot, start slowly. The muscles, tendons, and skin of your feet need time to adapt. Begin with short walks on soft grass or sandy beaches before progressing to rougher terrain. Over time, your feet will become stronger and more resilient, but it's important to listen to your body and avoid overdoing it.

Walking barefoot on the Earth can be a refreshing way to reconnect with nature and possibly enjoy health benefits associated with earthing. By practising environmental awareness, monitoring for hazards, and listening to your body, you can safely enjoy the practice of grounding while minimizing risks. Proper hygiene, knowledge of your surroundings, and gradual adaptation are key to a safe and enjoyable barefoot experience.

## Using grounding mats and sheets & cuffs

While walking barefoot outdoors is the most traditional method, many people seek to experience the potential benefits of grounding indoors, especially in urban or cold environments. For this purpose, a variety of grounding equipment has been developed, including grounding mats, sheets, and wrist cuffs. Here's an overview of each item and guidance on where to purchase them online.

## Grounding Mats

Grounding mats** are versatile, portable devices designed to mimic the Earth's surface by conducting its electric charge through a connection to a grounded power outlet or grounding rod. Made from conductive materials such as carbon-infused leatherette or polyurethane, grounding mats are typically placed on the floor under your bare feet, under your desk, or even on your bed.

How to Use:

To use a grounding mat, you simply plug its cord into the grounding port of a properly grounded electrical outlet or attach it to a grounding rod outside. Then, touch the mat with bare skin — most commonly with your feet or while resting your hands on it during work or relaxation.

Benefits:

Grounding mats are great for people who spend long hours indoors, offering a convenient way to maintain electrical contact with the Earth during work, sleep, or relaxation.

## Grounding Sheets

Grounding sheets** are bed sheets made with conductive silver threads woven throughout the fabric. When connected to a grounded outlet or rod, they allow the body to maintain continuous contact with the Earth's electrons while sleeping.

How to Use:

Lay the grounding sheet on your mattress like a regular fitted sheet. Plug the cord into a grounded outlet. As you sleep, your skin's contact with the sheet allows the transfer of electrons.

Benefits:

Grounding sheets are ideal for people interested in overnight grounding. Studies suggest sleeping grounded can help improve sleep quality, balance cortisol (the stress hormone), and reduce inflammation.

## Grounding Wrist Cuffs

Grounding wrist cuffs are adjustable bands, typically made of conductive materials, that wrap around the wrist or ankle. They are connected to the Earth via a cord and grounded outlet or rod.

How to Use:

Attach the cuff to your wrist or ankle and connect the cord to a grounded source. Wrist cuffs are lightweight and portable, making them suitable for use while working at a desk, reading, or watching TV.

Benefits:

Wrist cuffs are especially helpful for people who want targeted grounding and need to keep their hands and feet free.

## Where to Buy Grounding Equipment Online

A variety of reputable online outlets sell grounding mats, sheets, and wrist cuffs. Some of the most popular include:

1). Earthing.com**

(https://www.earthing.com)

Offers a wide range of grounding products, including mats, sheets, pillowcases, and bands. Founded by Clint Ober, a pioneer in grounding research.

2.Grounded.com**

(https://www.grounded.com)

Sells grounding mats, sheets, and accessories, with a focus on education and customer support.

3. Amazon

(https://www.amazon.com)

Features a broad selection of grounding products from various brands, allowing for price comparisons and customer reviews.

4. BioEnergy Products**

(https://bioenergyproducts.com)

UK-based supplier of grounding mats, sheets, and wrist bands with international shipping.

5. HealthyLine

(https://healthyline.com)

Offers grounding mats and products often combined with other wellness technologies, such as PEMF (pulsed electromagnetic field therapy).

6.Groundology

(https://www.groundology.com)

European supplier specializing in grounding equipment and accessories.

Grounding mats, sheets, and wrist cuffs provide convenient, practical ways to experience the potential benefits of earthing without needing to go outside. When purchased from reputable online outlets and used as directed, these tools can help bring the Earth's natural electrical connection into your home or workplace, supporting wellness routines year-round. Always follow safety guidelines, ensure your outlets are properly grounded, and consult product instructions for optimal use.

## Grounding in different environments

This simple practice can be done in a variety of natural environments, each offering unique sensory experiences and health benefits. Here's a look at some of the most popular natural settings for grounding, along with the specific advantages of each:

### 1.Grass Fields and Lawns

Description:

Grass is perhaps the most accessible surface for grounding. Parks, backyards, and sports fields provide soft, cool, and often pesticide-free grass that's gentle on bare feet.

Benefits:

Comfort: Grass cushions your feet, making it ideal for people new to grounding.

Stress Relief: The feeling of cool, moist grass can be calming and mood-lifting.

Accessibility: Urban dwellers can often find grassy areas in local parks, making regular grounding easy.

### 2. Beaches and Sandy Shores

Description:

Sandy beaches, whether by the sea, lakes, or rivers, offer a unique grounding environment. Both dry and wet sand conduct the Earth's energy, with wet sand being especially effective due to its higher mineral and moisture content.

Benefits:

Enhanced Electron Transfer: Wet sand and saltwater are excellent conductors, maximizing the flow of electrons.

Foot Massage: Walking on uneven sand stimulates pressure points on the feet, benefiting circulation and foot health.

Soothing Atmosphere: The rhythmic sound of waves and ocean air enhance relaxation and mental clarity.

### 3. Forests and Woodland Trails

Description:

Forests provide a grounding experience on soil, fallen leaves, moss, and sometimes exposed roots. The rich organic matter in forest soil is highly conductive.

Benefits:

Immersion in Nature: Forests offer "forest bathing," which, combined with grounding, can lower stress and blood pressure.

Fresh Air

Surrounded by trees, you benefit from cleaner, oxygen-rich air and natural aromatherapy from tree oils.

Connection to Biodiversity: The sights and sounds of wildlife add to the calming effect and sense of connection.

4. Riverbanks and Lakesides

Description:

The moist soil and pebbles along rivers and lakes are excellent for grounding, especially in areas with clean, natural water.

Benefits:

Superior Conductivity: Moisture-rich environments enhance electron absorption.

Cooling Effect: The proximity to water helps regulate body temperature during grounding.

Peaceful Setting: The gentle flow of water can enhance meditative states and mindfulness.

5. Rocky Outcrops and Mountains

Description:

Large rocks, boulders, and mountain surfaces—especially those with some moisture—can be used for earthing. Granite, basalt, and other minerals conduct Earth's energy well.

Benefits:

Unique Sensations: The texture and temperature of rocks provide sensory stimulation and grounding variety.

Scenic Views: Mountain vistas or rocky coastlines promote awe and emotional well-being.

Physical Challenge: Navigating rocks engages muscles, balance, and coordination.

6. **Gardens and Farmland**

Description:

Tending a garden or walking barefoot on freshly turned soil connects you directly to the Earth's surface.

Benefits:

Healing Microbes: Contact with soil introduces beneficial microbes, which may support immune health.

Productivity and Mindfulness: Gardening is associated with lower stress and increased feelings of accomplishment.

Year-Round Access: Gardens are often accessible at home, allowing frequent grounding opportunities.

From the soft comfort of a grassy park to the invigorating sensation of a rocky mountain, grounding can be practiced in a wide range of natural environments. Each setting not only facilitates electron absorption for potential health benefits like reduced inflammation and improved mood, but also offers unique sensory, psychological, and even spiritual rewards. By varying your grounding environments, you can enhance both your physical and emotional well-being while deepening your connection with the natural world.

# Benefits of Earthing

## The Health Benefits of Grounding/Earthing: Physical and Mental Well-being

While this concept may seem simple, a growing body of research and anecdotal evidence suggests that grounding can have significant benefits for both physical and mental health. Here's a comprehensive summary of the ways grounding is believed to support well-being.

### Physical Health Benefits

1. Reduced Inflammation and Pain

One of the most well-documented physical benefits of grounding is its anti-inflammatory effect. Chronic inflammation is a root cause of many modern diseases, including arthritis, heart disease, and diabetes. Grounding is thought to transfer electrons from the Earth into the body, which may neutralize free radicals and dampen inflammatory processes. Studies have shown that people who ground themselves after injury or strenuous exercise experience less pain, reduced muscle soreness, and faster recovery. This is particularly beneficial for athletes, those with chronic pain conditions, and anyone seeking natural relief from inflammation.

2. Improved Sleep Quality

Grounding has been linked to better sleep and normalized circadian rhythms. Research indicates that sleeping while grounded can help regulate cortisol, the stress hormone that influences the sleep-wake cycle. Participants in grounding studies often report falling asleep faster, experiencing deeper sleep, and waking feeling more refreshed. Better sleep is critical for immune function, cognitive performance, and overall physical health.

3. Enhanced Circulation and Cardiovascular Health

Grounding has been shown to improve blood flow and reduce blood viscosity, which is a risk factor for cardiovascular disease. By improving the electrical charge on red blood cells, grounding may help prevent clumping and clot formation, supporting heart health. Healthy circulation also means better oxygen and nutrient delivery throughout the body.

4. Faster Wound Healing

There is preliminary evidence that grounding may speed up the healing of wounds and injuries. This is likely linked to its anti-inflammatory and improved circulation effects, which help tissue repair and regeneration.

**Mental and Emotional Health Benefits**

1. Reduced Stress and Anxiety

Grounding is associated with lower levels of stress and anxiety. Direct contact with the Earth can calm the nervous system, reduce cortisol, and promote a sense of relaxation. Many people report feeling less "wired" or anxious after spending time barefoot in nature or using grounding equipment.

2. Improved Mood and Emotional Balance

Spending time in natural environments, especially when practising grounding, can boost mood and promote emotional well-being. The act of grounding itself, combined with exposure to sunlight, greenery, and fresh air, increases levels of endorphins and serotonin, the body's "feel-good" chemicals.

3. Enhanced Mindfulness and Connection

Grounding encourages mindfulness and a greater sense of connection—to both the Earth and oneself. This can foster a sense of presence, gratitude, and spiritual well-being. For those feeling disconnected or overwhelmed by technology, grounding offers a simple way to reconnect with the natural world.

Grounding is a natural, accessible practice that offers a range of physical and mental health benefits. By reducing inflammation, improving sleep, supporting cardiovascular health, and enhancing emotional well-being, grounding can be a valuable addition to a healthy lifestyle. Whether practiced outdoors or with grounding devices, spending time in contact with the Earth provides a profound sense of balance, vitality, and peace.

**Improved Sleep**

How Improved Sleep Might Happen with Earthing/Grounding Sheets, Mats, or Cuffs: The Physiology Behind It.

Sleep is a cornerstone of good health, affecting everything from immune function and hormone regulation to mental clarity and emotional stability. Many factors can disrupt sleep, including stress, chronic pain, inflammation, and irregularities in the body's internal clock. In recent years, the practice of earthing (grounding)—specifically using grounding sheets, mats, or wrist/ankle cuffs—has gained attention for its potential to improve sleep quality. But how might this simple practice lead to deeper, more restorative sleep? Let's explore the possible physiological mechanisms at play.

## The Physiology of Sleep Disruption

Before examining grounding's role, it's important to recognize why sleep can be disrupted. Modern life exposes us to artificial lighting, electronic devices, and electromagnetic fields (EMFs), all of which can interfere with natural circadian rhythms. Psychological stress, pain, and chronic inflammation can also elevate cortisol levels (the body's main stress hormone), making it harder to fall and stay asleep.

## The Role of Grounding in Sleep Physiology

1. Cortisol Regulation and the Circadian Rhythm

One of the most compelling scientific findings about grounding relates to cortisol, a hormone released by the adrenal glands in response to stress. Normally, cortisol levels follow a daily rhythm: they peak in the morning to wake us up and gradually decline throughout the day, reaching their lowest at night. Chronic stress or inflammation can disrupt this rhythm, leading to high night-time cortisol, which makes sleep elusive.

A landmark study by Ghaly and Teplitz (2004) found that people who slept on grounding (earthing) sheets for eight weeks had more normalized cortisol secretion patterns. Participants reported falling asleep faster, waking less often, and feeling more rested. The likely explanation is that grounding helps regulate the body's stress response, allowing for a smoother decline in cortisol at night and better alignment with the natural sleep-wake cycle.

2. Reduced Inflammation and Pain

Chronic low-grade inflammation and pain are major culprits in sleep disturbances. Grounding is thought to reduce inflammation by allowing the body to absorb free electrons from the Earth, which neutralize reactive oxygen species (free radicals) and dampen inflammatory responses. With less inflammation and pain, the body can relax more easily, and sleep becomes deeper and less fragmented.

3. Calming the Nervous System

Grounding may also modulate the autonomic nervous system, shifting it toward a parasympathetic ("rest and digest") state. This is the opposite of the sympathetic ("fight or flight") state that is dominant during stress. Some studies on grounding mats have shown improvements in heart rate variability—a sign of reduced stress and improved relaxation—which can make it easier to fall asleep and stay asleep through the night.

4. Reduction in EMF-Related Sleep Disruption

Modern environments are saturated with EMFs from electronics and wiring. Some researchers hypothesize that grounding helps discharge the body's accumulated static electricity and may protect against potential sleep-disrupting effects of EMFs, though more research is needed in this area.

**How to Use Grounding Products for Sleep**

Grounding sheets are woven with silver or carbon fibres and are connected to a grounded outlet, allowing continuous electron transfer during sleep. Mats can be placed under fitted sheets or at your feet, and wrist/ankle cuffs allow targeted grounding. For best results, maintain direct skin contact with the grounding surface.

Grounding sheets, mats, and cuffs may improve sleep by regulating stress hormones, reducing inflammation and pain, calming the nervous system, and potentially shielding against EMFs. By supporting the body's natural physiology, earthing offers a simple, non-pharmacological approach to achieving more restful and restorative sleep.

## Reduced inflammation and pain

Just how Earthing/Grounding Can Reduce Inflammation and Pain:
## Exploring the Physiological Process

Earthing, also known as grounding, is the practice of making direct physical contact with the Earth's surface—such as walking barefoot on grass, soil, sand, or using grounding devices indoors. Increasingly, scientific studies and anecdotal reports suggest that earthing may help reduce inflammation and pain in the body. But how could such a simple act have such profound effects on our physiology? To answer this, we must look at the interplay between the body's electrical state, the Earth's electrons, and the mechanisms underlying inflammation and pain.

## The Body's Electrical State and Inflammation

The human body is an electrical organism: cells communicate using electrical signals, and many biochemical processes rely on the movement of charged particles. Inflammation—a natural immune response to injury or infection—produces substances known as reactive oxygen species (ROS), or free radicals. These are highly reactive molecules with unpaired electrons. Their purpose is to destroy pathogens and initiate tissue repair, but when produced in excess or not neutralized, they can cause collateral damage to healthy tissues. This results in chronic inflammation and pain, contributing to diseases such as arthritis, cardiovascular disease, and autoimmune disorders.

## The Earth's Free Electrons: Nature's Antioxidant

The Earth's surface possesses a virtually unlimited supply of free electrons. When direct skin contact is made with the ground, electrons can flow from the Earth into the body. Grounding devices (such as mats and sheets) plugged into grounded outlets can also facilitate this transfer. These electrons are nature's original antioxidants—they can neutralize ROS by pairing with their unpaired electrons, thus reducing oxidative stress and the inflammatory response.

## Physiological Processes Involved

1. Neutralization of Free Radicals

When grounding occurs, the influx of electrons into the body can directly interact with and neutralize ROS. This reduces oxidative damage to healthy cells and tissues, halting the cycle of chronic inflammation. By restoring a balanced electrical state, the body's tissues are less prone to the persistent irritation that underlies many pain conditions.

2. Reduced Inflammatory Markers

Several studies have found that grounding can lower blood levels of markers associated with inflammation, such as C-reactive protein and white blood cell counts. For example, research on subjects recovering from exercise-induced muscle damage showed faster recovery, less pain, and reduced swelling when the subjects were grounded. These findings suggest that grounding not only mitigates initial inflammation but also accelerates the resolution phase, helping the body return to a baseline state more quickly.

3. Improved Blood Flow and Reduced Viscosity

Inflammation is closely linked to blood viscosity (thickness) and circulation. Grounding has been shown to improve the zeta potential (electrical charge) of red blood cells, making them less likely to clump together. This leads to smoother blood flow, better oxygen delivery, and more efficient removal of waste products from tissues—factors that reduce pain and promote healing.

4. Modulation of the Nervous System**

Chronic pain is often amplified by heightened activity of the sympathetic nervous system ("fight or flight" response). Grounding appears to shift the body toward parasympathetic dominance ("rest and repair"), promoting relaxation, lowering stress hormones, and reducing pain perception.

Earthing/grounding reduces inflammation and pain through a combination of physiological processes: neutralizing excess free radicals, lowering inflammatory markers, improving blood flow, and calming the nervous system. By restoring the body's electrical balance and supporting its innate healing mechanisms, grounding offers a simple, natural way to combat chronic inflammation and pain, with both preventative and therapeutic potential.

**Enhanced immune function**

How Earthing/Grounding Can Enhance the Body's Immune Function: The Link Between Negatively Charged Particles and the Immune System

Earthing, or grounding, describes the practice of making direct physical contact with the Earth's surface—through bare feet, hands, or specialized conductive devices. Over the past two decades, emerging research has suggested that grounding may support a wide range of health benefits, including enhanced immune function. Understanding how this happens requires a look at the body's electrical nature, the role of negatively charged particles (electrons), and the mechanisms of immune regulation.

## The Human Body, Electrons, and Immunity

The human body is a complex bioelectrical system. Many physiological processes, including those of the immune system, rely on the movement of electrons and maintenance of electrical gradients across cell membranes. The immune response, especially during inflammation, involves the generation of highly reactive molecules called free radicals or reactive oxygen species (ROS). These molecules are essential for destroying pathogens and damaged cells, but if not kept in balance, they can also damage healthy tissue and perpetuate chronic inflammation.

The Earth's surface is a natural reservoir of free electrons (negatively charged particles). Direct contact with the Earth allows the body to absorb these electrons, which can influence cellular and systemic functions— including those of the immune system.

## Ways Grounding Enhances Immune Function

1. Neutralization of Excess Free Radicals

During immune activity—such as fighting infections or repairing injuries— white blood cells produce ROS to destroy invaders. However, excess ROS can lead to oxidative stress, damaging healthy cells and causing chronic inflammation, which in turn can impair immune efficiency and promote disease.

Grounding allows electrons from the Earth to enter the body and neutralize excess ROS by pairing with their unpaired electrons. This process, called "electron donation," helps prevent unnecessary tissue damage and chronic inflammation. By reducing oxidative stress, the immune system operates more efficiently, focusing its activity where it is truly needed.

2. Modulation of Inflammatory Responses

Chronic, unresolved inflammation can exhaust the immune system and is a risk factor for many diseases, from autoimmune disorders to cancer. Research has shown that grounding reduces blood markers of inflammation, such as C-reactive protein and pro-inflammatory cytokines. This modulation of the inflammatory response allows the immune system to return to a balanced, vigilant state, rather than remaining in a state of chronic activation.

3. Improved Circulation and Tissue Oxygenation

Effective immune responses depend on good blood flow, which delivers immune cells to sites of injury or infection and removes metabolic waste. Grounding has been shown to decrease blood viscosity (thickness), reducing the tendency of red blood cells to clump. This improves micro-circulation, ensuring that immune cells can travel efficiently throughout the body, enhancing surveillance and rapid response to pathogens.

4. Balancing the Autonomic Nervous System

The autonomic nervous system (ANS) regulates many immune functions. Chronic stress and sympathetic overdrive ("fight or flight") can suppress immune activity, making the body more susceptible to illness. Grounding appears to shift the ANS toward parasympathetic dominance ("rest and repair"), which supports optimal immune function, reduces stress hormones like cortisol, and fosters recovery.

## Scientific Evidence and Observations

Pilot studies and anecdotal reports have indicated that people who practice grounding regularly experience fewer infections, quicker recovery from illness, and less severe allergic or autoimmune reactions. Some studies have also shown that grounding increases the activity of certain immune cells, like natural killer cells, and enhances the resolution of inflammation after injury.

The influx of negatively charged particles (electrons) from the Earth acts as a powerful, natural antioxidant defence, supporting the immune system's ability to respond to threats efficiently while minimizing collateral tissue damage. As research grows, grounding is emerging as a simple, accessible strategy for bolstering immune resilience and supporting overall health.

## Stress reduction and well-being

The Link Between Earthing/Grounding and Stress Reduction & Well-being: Biological and Hormonal Mechanisms

Earthing, or grounding, is the practice of making direct physical contact with the Earth's surface—whether through bare feet on grass, sand, or soil, or via conductive devices like mats and sheets indoors. While many people report feeling calmer and more centred after grounding, scientific research is beginning to reveal the biological and hormonal pathways through which this simple practice may reduce stress and promote overall well-being.

## The Biological Stress Response

•Stress, whether acute or chronic, triggers a cascade of physiological changes in the body. The central axis of the stress response involves the hypothalamus-pituitary-adrenal (HPA) axis and the sympathetic ("fight or flight") branch of the autonomic nervous system. When a person is stressed:

The hypothalamus signals the pituitary gland to release adrenocorticotropic hormone (ACTH).

ACTH stimulates the adrenal glands to release cortisol, the body's primary stress hormone.

Sympathetic nerves release adrenaline and noradrenaline, increasing heart rate and blood pressure.

Chronic activation of this pathway can disrupt sleep, impair immune function, increase inflammation, and contribute to anxiety, depression, and other health problems.

## How Grounding Affects Stress Biology

1. Cortisol Regulation

Cortisol is essential for managing acute stress, but chronically elevated cortisol is harmful to health. Studies have shown that grounding can normalize cortisol secretion. For instance, a landmark study by Ghaly and Teplitz (2004) found that people who slept on grounded sheets exhibited more natural, diurnal rhythms of cortisol, with levels peaking in the morning and declining at night—corresponding to improved sleep and reduced stress. This suggests that grounding may help reset the body's internal clock and buffer the physiological impacts of chronic stress.

2. Autonomic Nervous System Balance

The autonomic nervous system (ANS) has two main branches: sympathetic (arousing) and parasympathetic (calming). Chronic stress keeps the body locked in sympathetic mode, which is linked to anxiety, high blood pressure, and poor digestion.

Research using grounding mats has shown that subjects experience increased heart rate variability (HRV) when grounded. HRV is a marker of greater parasympathetic ("rest and digest") activity and overall resilience to stress. By promoting parasympathetic dominance, grounding helps the body recover from stress, enhances relaxation, and fosters a sense of calm and well-being.

3. Reduction of Inflammation and Oxidative Stress**

Stress and inflammation are tightly interlinked: stress hormones like cortisol can promote inflammation, and inflammation can, in turn, perpetuate stress. Grounding allows electrons from the Earth to neutralize free radicals produced during stress and inflammation, breaking this vicious cycle. Lower inflammation means less physical and psychological strain on the body, leading to a greater sense of well-being.

4. Improved Sleep Quality

Chronic stress disrupts sleep, and poor sleep amplifies stress—a harmful feedback loop. By normalizing cortisol and calming the nervous system, grounding can improve sleep quality, which in turn increases resilience to everyday stressors and boosts mood.

Psychological and Subjective Well-being

Alongside measurable biological changes, grounding often produces subjective feelings of relaxation, reduced anxiety, improved mood, and greater connection to nature. These effects may arise from both physiological processes and the sensory, mindful experience of direct contact with the Earth.

Earthing/grounding reduces stress and enhances well-being by influencing key biological and hormonal systems: it regulates cortisol, shifts the autonomic nervous system toward relaxation, reduces inflammation, and improves sleep. Together, these effects create a powerful support system for physical and psychological health, making grounding a simple yet effective practice for managing modern stress and promoting holistic well-being.

# Safety Tips and Considerations

## When and Where to Ground Safely: Guidelines for Setting Up or Starting Earthing / Grounding

While the practice is generally safe for most people, knowing when and where to ground is important to maximize benefits and minimize risks. Here's a comprehensive guide to safe grounding, whether you're starting outdoors or using grounding devices inside.

### When to Ground

1. Any Time of Day:

 Morning: Grounding in the morning can help wake you up, regulate your circadian rhythm, and set a positive tone for the day.

 Afternoon: A midday grounding session can reduce stress and fatigue, especially if you spend long hours indoors or at a computer.

 Evening: Grounding in the evening may promote relaxation and help you unwind before bed, potentially improving sleep quality.

2. After Physical Activity:

Grounding post-exercise can help reduce muscle soreness, speed up recovery, and decrease inflammation.

3. During Periods of Stress or Illness:

If you're feeling anxious, overwhelmed, or under the weather, grounding may help calm your nervous system and support immune function.

## Where to Ground Outdoors Safely

1. Grass:

Ideal Locations: Parks, backyards, gardens, and sports fields with clean, pesticide-free grass.

Benefits: Soft surface, usually free from sharp objects, and often accessible for regular grounding.

2. Beach or Sand:

Ideal Locations: Seashores, lake-fronts, riverbanks with clean sand.

Benefits: Sand, especially when wet, is highly conductive and provides a pleasant sensory experience.

3. Soil or Dirt:

Ideal Locations: Forest trails, gardens, or natural earth patches.

Benefits: Rich in minerals, highly conductive, and offers a grounding connection.

4. Avoid Risky Areas:

Urban settings with potential for glass, metal, or chemical contamination.

Areas with hazardous plants such as poison ivy or poison oak.

Sites with excessive animal waste or parasites.

## Safety Tips:

Inspect the ground for sharp objects, debris, or animal droppings.

Know local flora and fauna to avoid allergic reactions or bites.

- Watch weather conditions:** Avoid grounding outdoors during storms or when the ground is frozen, extremely hot, or unsafe due to lightning risk.

Where to Ground Indoors Safely

1. Grounding Mats, Sheets, or Bands:

Use certified products** from reputable suppliers.

Plug into a properly grounded outlet** (test with a ground tester before use).

Place mats** under your feet at a desk, on the floor, or under your bed sheet.

Use wrist or ankle bands** for targeted grounding while reading or working.

2. Safety Precautions:

Ensure outlets are grounded**—use a socket tester before plugging in grounding equipment.

Follow product instructions** for set-up, care, and cleaning.

Consult your doctor** if you have a pacemaker, are pregnant, or have a chronic health condition.

**When Not to Ground**

During thunderstorms: Avoid outdoor grounding to prevent the risk of lightning strikes.

On contaminated ground: Steer clear of areas with chemical spills, heavy pollution, or biohazards.

If you have open wounds or skin infections: Protect yourself from potential pathogens in soil or sand.

Choose clean, natural surfaces outdoors, or use certified grounding products indoors. Always inspect your grounding area or equipment, and consider your own health status when starting or setting up your grounding routine. With these guidelines, you can enjoy the benefits of earthing while minimizing risks to your safety and well-being.

# Conclusion

## Conclusion:

As we have explored throughout this book, earthing—or grounding—offers a profound yet beautifully simple way to support physical and mental well-being. In our modern world, we are often disconnected from the natural environment that once formed the backdrop of daily life. Concrete, synthetic flooring, and endless hours indoors have erected barriers between our bodies and the subtle, life-affirming energies of the Earth. Yet, science is now catching up with ancient wisdom, revealing that our need for direct contact with the ground is more than just a matter of comfort or tradition—it is a biological necessity.

The benefits of earthing, as reviewed across research studies and personal accounts, are wide-ranging and compelling. Physically, grounding has been shown to reduce inflammation, lessen pain, improve sleep quality, regulate cortisol and stress hormones, enhance circulation, speed up healing, and support immune function. At the molecular level, this is largely attributed to the transfer of free electrons from the Earth into the body, which act as natural antioxidants—neutralizing harmful free radicals and interrupting cycles of chronic inflammation and oxidative stress.

Mentally and emotionally, earthing offers a sanctuary from the relentless pace and pressures of modern life. Regular grounding—whether by walking barefoot in a park, gardening, relaxing on the beach, or using grounding devices indoors—has been linked to reduced anxiety, better mood, increased mental clarity, and a greater sense of connection and calm. These benefits may be mediated by physiological changes in the nervous and endocrine systems, but they are also deeply experiential, arising from mindful moments of reconnection with nature.

The science behind earthing is still evolving, but the body of evidence is growing. While some studies are preliminary or small in scale, their results are promising and consistently point toward meaningful health effects. Researchers have measured changes in blood markers of inflammation, cortisol rhythms, heart rate variability, wound healing, and even blood viscosity—all showing improvement with regular grounding. Future research, especially large-scale, placebo-controlled trials, will be critical in further validating these findings and clarifying the underlying mechanisms.

As you reach the end of this book, the invitation is simple: try earthing for yourself. No special equipment or advanced knowledge is required—just a willingness to take off your shoes, step outside, and let your skin touch the living Earth. Notice how your body feels, how your mind responds, and how your mood shifts. If outdoor grounding is not always convenient, consider using grounding mats, sheets, or cuffs as described in previous chapters.

Looking ahead, the future of earthing research is bright. As more people seek natural, accessible ways to support health and resilience, grounding offers a low-cost, low-risk intervention with the potential for profound impact. Scientists are already exploring its applications in sleep, chronic pain, cardiovascular health, mental health, and immune function. With growing awareness and clinical interest, we may soon see earthing integrated into mainstream wellness and healthcare.

In a world of ever-increasing complexity, earthing reminds us that sometimes, the simplest solutions are right beneath our feet. Whether for a moment of peace or a lifetime of well-being, the ground is always there —waiting for us to return.

## Appendices

## Appendices

## Frequently Asked Questions (FAQs) About Earthing/Grounding

Q: What is earthing or grounding?

A: Earthing, or grounding, is the practice of making direct physical contact with the Earth's surface (such as soil, grass, sand, or water) or using conductive devices indoors to connect the body to the Earth's natural electric charge.

Q: How long should I practice earthing to see benefits?

A: While some people notice benefits (such as relaxation or pain relief) after just one session, most studies suggest 20–40 minutes daily provides meaningful results. Consistency is key for long-term benefits.

Q: Can I ground myself indoors?

A: Yes. Special products like grounding mats, sheets, and wrist/ankle bands connect to a grounded outlet or grounding rod, allowing you to experience earthing indoors.

Q: Is earthing safe for everyone?

A: Generally, yes. However, individuals with electronic medical implants (like pacemakers) or certain health conditions should consult their healthcare provider before using grounding devices.

Q: What surfaces are best for earthing?

A: Moist grass, soil, sand, and unpainted concrete are excellent. Wood, asphalt, and most carpets do not conduct the Earth's energy well.

Q: Can I practice earthing in the winter?

A: Yes, but be mindful of cold temperatures and slippery surfaces. Indoor grounding devices are a good alternative during harsh weather.

Q: How do I know if my indoor outlet is properly grounded?

A: Use a simple outlet tester (available online) to check for a safe ground connection before plugging in any grounding equipment.

## Resources and Where to Find Grounding Products

Online Retailers:

- [Earthing.com](https://www.earthing.com): Comprehensive range of official grounding mats, sheets, and accessories.

- [Groundology.com](https://www.groundology.com): Europe-based supplier with international shipping.

- [Grounded.com](https://www.grounded.com): Offers grounding products and educational resources.

- [Amazon](https://www.amazon.com): Multiple brands and product reviews for comparison.

- [BioEnergy Products](https://bioenergyproducts.com): UK-based, offers mats, sheets, and wrist/ankle bands.

- [HealthyLine](https://healthyline.com): Focuses on grounding mats, sometimes combined with other wellness technologies.

## Educational Resources:

Earthing: The Most Important Health Discovery Ever?* by Clinton Ober, Stephen T. Sinatra, and Martin Zucker.

- [The Earthing Institute](https://earthinginstitute.net): Research, articles, and FAQs on grounding science and practice.

- Peer-reviewed journals (e.g., *Journal of Environmental and Public Health*, *Journal of Inflammation Research*) for scientific studies.

## Simple Experiments to Experience Earthing

1. The Barefoot Comparison

Materials Your feet, grassy or sandy surface, timer.

Instructions: Spend 30 minutes barefoot on grass or sand. Note your mood, pain level, or energy before and after. Try the same activity the next day with shoes on and compare your experience.

2. Sleep Quality Test

Materials: Grounding sheet or mat, journal.

Instructions: Use a grounding sheet or mat on your bed for one week. Each morning, record your sleep quality, how quickly you fell asleep, and how you feel on waking. Compare with a week sleeping without grounding.

3. Stress and Heart Rate

Materials: Grounding mat, timer, phone or fitness tracker (optional for HR).

Instructions:Sit quietly with bare feet on a grounding mat for 20 minutes. Track your heart rate before and after, and note your mental state and stress level. Repeat for several days and observe patterns.

4. Post-Exercise Muscle Soreness

Materials: Grounding mat or patch.

Instructions: After a workout, ground yourself for 30 minutes. Track muscle soreness over the next 48 hours and compare with a post-workout routine without grounding.

5. Indoor vs. Outdoor Grounding

Materials:** Grounding mat, grassy area.

Instructions: Spend equal time grounding inside (mat) and outside (barefoot). Reflect on differences in physical sensations and emotional state.

**Remember:**

Document your results, listen to your body, and consult a healthcare provider if you have underlying medical conditions. With curiosity and mindfulness, these experiments can help you discover the potential benefits of earthing for yourself.

## Glossary

Key terms explained in simple language

## Glossary of Terms

Antioxidants

Substances that help protect the body's cells from damage caused by free radicals. They can be found in foods or absorbed from the Earth's surface through grounding.

Autonomic Nervous System (ANS)

The part of the nervous system that controls automatic body functions like heartbeat, breathing, and digestion. It has two main branches: sympathetic (fight or flight) and parasympathetic (rest and digest).

Cortisol

A hormone released by the adrenal glands in response to stress. It helps control blood sugar, metabolism, and the sleep-wake cycle.

Earthing (Grounding)

The practice of making direct physical contact with the Earth's surface, or using conductive devices indoors, to connect the body to the Earth's natural electric charge.

Electrons

Tiny negatively charged particles found in atoms. Free electrons from the Earth can enter the body during grounding, acting as natural antioxidants.

Electromagnetic Fields (EMFs)

Invisible areas of energy often produced by electrical devices, wiring, and wireless technology. Some people believe EMFs can affect health, and grounding may help reduce their impact.

Free Radicals (Reactive Oxygen Species/ROS)

Highly reactive molecules with unpaired electrons that can damage the body's cells. They are produced by normal metabolism, stress, or inflammation.

Grounding Devices

Products like mats, sheets, wrist/ankle bands, and patches that allow a person to connect to the Earth's energy indoors by plugging into a grounded outlet or using a grounding rod.

Grounding Outlet

A special part of most wall outlets connected to the Earth, used to safely transfer the Earth's energy to indoor grounding devices.

Heart Rate Variability (HRV)

A measure of the variation in time between each heartbeat. Higher HRV is generally a sign of better stress resilience and autonomic nervous system balance.

Inflammation

The body's natural response to injury, infection, or harmful substances. Chronic inflammation can cause pain and contribute to many diseases.

Oxidative Stress

A condition that happens when there are too many free radicals in the body and not enough antioxidants to neutralize them. It can damage cells and is linked to ageing and disease.

Parasympathetic Nervous System

The part of the autonomic nervous system that helps the body relax, recover, and digest food. Often called the "rest and digest" system.

Red Blood Cells

Cells in the blood that carry oxygen from the lungs to the rest of the body. Their electrical charge helps them flow smoothly and not stick together.

Sympathetic Nervous System

The part of the autonomic nervous system that prepares the body for action, stress, or danger. Often called the "fight or flight" system.

White Blood Cells

Cells in the immune system that help fight infections and remove damaged cells from the body.

This glossary provides simple explanations for key terms you'll encounter in the world of earthing and grounding. Understanding these concepts can help you make the most of your grounding practice and appreciate the science behind it.

# References

1. Chevalier, G., Sinatra, S. T., Oschman, J. L., Sokal, K., & Sokal, P. (2012). Earthing: Health implications of reconnecting the human body to the Earth's surface electrons. *Journal of Environmental and Public Health*, 2012, Article ID 291541. https://doi.org/10.1155/2012/291541

2. Ghaly, M., & Teplitz, D. (2004). The biologic effects of grounding the human body during sleep as measured by cortisol levels and subjective reporting of sleep, pain, and stress. *Journal of Alternative and Complementary Medicine*, 10(5), 767–776. https://doi.org/10.1089/acm.2004.10.767

3. Brown, D., Chevalier, G., & Hill, M. (2010). Pilot study on the effect of grounding on delayed-onset muscle soreness. *Journal of Alternative and Complementary Medicine*, 16(3), 265–273. https://doi.org/10.1089/acm.2009.0399

4. Oschman, J. L. (2007). *Energy Medicine: The Scientific Basis* (2nd ed.). Elsevier.

5. Ober, C., Sinatra, S. T., & Zucker, M. (2010). *Earthing: The Most Important Health Discovery Ever?* Basic Health Publications.

6. Sokal, K., & Sokal, P. (2011). Earthing the human body influences physiologic processes. *Journal of Alternative and Complementary Medicine*, 17(4), 301–308. https://doi.org/10.1089/acm.2010.0687

7. The Earthing Institute. (n.d.). *Earthing Research and Resources*. https://earthinginstitute.net/

8. Oschman, J. L., Chevalier, G., & Brown, R. (2015). The effects of grounding (Earthing) on inflammation, the immune response, wound

healing, and prevention and treatment of chronic inflammatory and autoimmune diseases. In S. M. Paul (Ed.), *Advances in Integrative Medicine* (pp. 1–8). Elsevier.

9. Terman, M., & Terman, J. S. (2005). Light therapy for seasonal and nonseasonal depression: Efficacy, protocol, safety, and side effects. *CNS Spectrums*, 10(8), 647–663.

10. National Institutes of Health. (n.d.). Free radicals and antioxidants: How do they work? https://www.nih.gov/news-events/nih-research-matters/free-radicals-antioxidants-how-they-work

END

Printed in Dunstable, United Kingdom

66606742R00057